for the

D0284697

Other giftbooks by Helen Exley:
In Praise and Celebration of Friendship
Thank you for every little thing
Words on Love and Caring
Words on Kindness
An Illustrated Friendship Notebook
I wish you Happiness!

Published simultaneously in 1998 by Exley Publications in
Great Britain, and Exley Publications LLC in the USA.
Copyright © Helen Exley 1998
The moral right of the author has been asserted.

12 11 10 9 8 7 6 5 4 3

ISBN 1-86187-044-2

Quotations selected by Helen Exley.
Illustrated by Angela Kerr.
Printed in China.

**Exley Publications Ltd, 16 Chalk Hill, Watford,
Herts WD1 4BN, UK.
Exley Publications LLC, 232 Madison Avenue,
Suite 1409, NY 10016, USA.**

A *Friend* IS FOREVER

A HELEN EXLEY GIFTBOOK

≣ EXLEY
NEW YORK • WATFORD, UK

*With a friend at your
side no road
seems too long.*

JAPANESE PROVERB

*Friendship improves
happiness, and abates
misery, by doubling our
joy, and dividing
our grief.*

JOSEPH ADDISON

*We have been
friends together;
in sunshine
and in shade.*

CAROLINE NORTON

*One's friends are
that part of the
human race with
which one can
be human.*

GEORGE SANTAYANA

May friendship like wine, improve as time advances. And may we always have old wine, old friends, and young cares.

TRADITIONAL

A friend hears
the song in my
heart and sings it
to me when my
memory fails.

FROM "PIONEER GIRLS
LEADERS' HANDBOOK"

That is the best – to laugh with someone because you both think the same things are funny.

GLORIA VANDERBILT

The proper office of a friend is to side with you when you are in the wrong. Nearly anybody will side with you when you are in the right.

MARK TWAIN

Best friend,
my well-spring
in the wilderness.

GEORGE ELIOT
(MARY ANN EVANS)

No one can develop freely in this world and find a full life without feeling understood by at least one person.

PAUL TOURNIER

*Hold a true friend
with both your hands.*

NIGERIAN PROVERB

*[Friends] stand there
as a solid and
impregnable bulwark
against all the evils
of life.*

SYDNEY SMITH

*The test of friendship
is assistance
in adversity, and that,
too, unconditional
assistance.*

MAHATMA GANDHI

Silences make the real conversations between friends. Not the saying but the never needing to say is what counts.

MARGARET LEE RUNBECK

Of all the things which wisdom provides to make life entirely happy, much the greatest is the possession of friendship.

EPICURUS

A mile walked with a friend contains only a hundred steps.

RUSSIAN PROVERB

*True friends
are those
seeking solitude
together.*

ABEL BONNARD

A friend, by a phone call, a popping-in, a chance meeting, a small unexpected surprise, puts a little jam on the day's bread and butter.

J . R . C .

*F*riendship is the only
cement that will ever
hold the world together.

WOODROW WILSON

*T*here is nothing final
between friends.

WILLIAM BRYAN

Knowing you are somewhere – near or far – means I'm never, never totally alone.

MARION C. GARRETTY

*In
prosperity
our friends
know us;
In adversity
we know
our friends.*

J.M. BARRIE

*In a thousand ways
[my friends] have turned
my limitations into
beautiful privileges, and
enabled me to walk
serene and happy in the
shadow cast by my
deprivation.*

HELEN KELLER

When you meet a man, you judge him by his clothes; When you leave, you judge him by his heart.

RUSSIAN PROVERB

Friendships that have stood the test of time and change are surely best.

JOSEPH PARRY

*We need friendship
all the time, just as
much as we need the
proverbial prime
necessities of life,
fire and water.*

CICERO

A friend is a person with whom I may be sincere. Before him I may think aloud.

RALPH WALDO EMERSON

The language of friendship is not words but meanings.

HENRY DAVID THOREAU

So long as we are loved by others, we are indispensable; and no man is useless while he has a friend.

ROBERT LOUIS STEVENSON

Nothing
can
come
between
true
friends.

EURIPIDES

Friends do not live in harmony merely, as some say, but in melody.

HENRY DAVID THOREAU

*Each friend represents
a world in us,
a world possibly not
born until they arrive,
and it is only by this
meeting that a new
world is born.*

ANAÏS NIN

*We do not mind
our not arriving
anywhere nearly so
much as our not
having any company
on the way.*

FRANK MOORE COLBY

Wherever you are it is your own friends who make your world.

WILLIAM JAMES

*Friendships link
and loop and interweave
until they mesh the world.*

PAM BROWN

*In my friend,
I find a
second self.*

ISABEL NORTON

A friend knows how

to allow for mere

quantity in your talk,

and only replies

to the quality....

WILLIAM DEAN HOWELLS

Seeing a good friend is like going home, or like tasting Mother's cooking. I feel secure, and need not protect myself. "Here," I say, "it is safe, for I am loved."

ARNOLD R. BEISSER

As long as there is a
post and the telephone is
not cut off, so long as we
have things to tell and
joys and anxieties to share –
we will be friends.

MARION C. GARRETTY

*Friendship multiplies
the good of life and
divides the evil. 'Tis the
sole remedy against
misfortune, the very
ventilation of the soul.*

BALTASAR GRACIAN

*What is
a friend?
A single soul
dwelling in
two bodies.*

ARISTOTLE

There's nothing
worth the wear
of winning,
but laughter and
the love of friends.

HILAIRE BELLOC

... friendship, the ease of it, it is not something to be taken lightly – nor for granted. Because, after breathing and eating and sleeping, friendships are essential to our survival.

ADELAIDE BRY

*W*hen friendship once

is rooted fast

It is a plant

no storm can blast.

FROM A 19TH-CENTURY
CALLING CARD

We are not primarily put on the earth to see through one another, but to see one another through.

PETER DE VRIES

*Trouble is a sieve
through which we
sift our acquaintances.
Those too big to
pass through are
our friends.*

ARLENE FRANCIS

When a friend asks there is no tomorrow.

GEORGE HERBERT

I trust that even when I'm out of sight I'm not out of mind. Silences and distances are woven into the texture of every true friendship.

ROBERTA ISRAELOFF

*Friends, companions,
lovers, are those
who treat us in terms
of our unlimited worth
to ourselves.*

HENRY ALONZO MYERS

[Friends] are closest to us who best understand what life means to us, who feel for us as we feel for ourselves, who are bound to us in triumph and disaster, who break the spell of our loneliness.

HENRY ALONZO MYERS

A friend is the one
who comes in when
the whole world has
gone out.

ALBAN GOODIER

*If you accompany
a friend, there is
no detour too far.*

LEO TOLSTOY

Grief can take care of itself, but to get the full value of a joy you must have somebody to divide it with.

MARK TWAIN

*T*he most I can
do for my friend
is simply to be
his friend.

HENRY DAVID THOREAU

True friendship comes

when silence between

two people is

comfortable.

DAVE TYSON GENTRY

What do we live for, if it is not to make life less difficult for each other?

GEORGE ELIOT
(MARY ANN EVANS)

Friendship is unnecessary, like philosopy, like art... It has no survival value; rather it is one of those things that give value to survival.

C. S. LEWIS

The bird a nest,
the spider a web,
man friendship.

WILLIAM BLAKE

*Happiness
seems made
to be shared.*

JEAN RACINE

*Friendship's
the wine
of life.*

EDWARD YOUNG

Friendship without
self-interest is one of
the rare and beautiful
things of life.

JAMES BYRNES

Wishing to be friends
is quick work,
but friendship is a
slow-ripening fruit.

ARISTOTLE

*Friendship
is a
sheltering
tree.*

SAMUEL TAYLOR COLERIDGE

Your friend is the man who knows all about you, and still likes you.

ELBERT HUBBARD

*Friendship, a dear
balm...
A smile among dark
frowns: a beloved light:
A solitude, a refuge, a
delight.*

PERCY BYSSHE SHELLEY

One can do

without people,

but one has

need of a friend.

CHINESE PROVERB

*Cooperation
is spelled
with two
letters: we.*

G.M. VERITY

It is one of the
blessings of old
friends that you
can afford to be
stupid with them.

RALPH WALDO EMERSON

I always felt that the great high privilege, relief and comfort of friendship was that one had to explain nothing.

KATHERINE MANSFIELD

Friend derives from a word meaning "free". A friend is someone who allows us the space and freedom to be.

DEBBIE ALICEN

*My friend is
one who likes
me for what
I am.*

HENRY DAVID THOREAU

To have even one good friend is to keep the darkness at bay.

PAM BROWN

Trouble shared is trouble halved.

DOROTHY SAYERS

... True Blue Friends...

make you feel good

and warm; they are

automatically on the

same wavelength.

ADELAIDE BRY

*Don't walk in front of me, I may not follow.
Don't walk behind me, I may not lead.
Walk beside me, and just be my friend.*

ALBERT CAMUS

For whoever knows how to return a kindness he has received must be a friend above all price.

SOPHOCLES

When a person
that one loves is
in the world and
alive and well...
then to miss them
is only a new
flavour, a salt
sharpness in
experience.

WINIFRED HOLTBY

What is a friend?
I will tell you.
It is a person with
whom you dare to
be yourself.

FRANK CRANE

*O*ld friends are best. King James used to call for his old shoes; they were easiest for his feet.

JOHN SELDON

*Because I got you
to look after me,
and you got me
to look after
you....
We got each other,
that's what,
that gives
a hoot in hell
about us....*

JOHN STEINBECK

To your
good health,
old friend,
may you live
for a
thousand years,
and I be there
to count them.

ROBERT SMITH SURTEES